HAROLD PATTER AND THE ~~CURSED~~ WORST CHILD

BY JOHN MARQUANE

Reviews for
Harold Patter and the Worst Child

"This play is the perfect read for any Harold Patter fan with a strong knack for visualizing things that they see described in words."
    -- Harold Pinter

"For all those readers who have always wondered: *What happens next?* This play provides all the dull, unimaginative answers."
    --Harold Bloom

"J. K. Rowling has done it again! Wait, whose name was that? Who did you say wrote pretty much all of it?"
    -- Harry Reid

"All of the friendship and magic fans have grown up loving from world-famous fantasy writer JACK THORNE."
    -- Harrison Ford

"When I gave this book to my granddaughter she said it was the one she wanted for her birthday and totally, totally not a different one."
    -- My friend Harold

"Both longtime fans and newcomers to the world of Harold Patter will be delighted by the wide margins and large line breaks that comprise this latest installment."
    -- J. K. Rowling

HAROLD PATTER AND THE WORST CHILD

CONTENTS

ACT I

* * *

ACT I, SCENE I

* * *

KING'S CROSS TRAIN STATION

Your typical London train station: it's soggy and it stinks. Two young boys, JIMMY and ELBOWS, pull huge suitcases. Their mother, GINGER, chases after them. Behind her walks, at a comfortable pace, the man himself, the boy who lived: HAROLD PATTER.

ELBOWS: Make him shut up!

HAROLD: What's all this about?

JIMMY: I'm just saying he's going to end up in Grumpindor.

HAROLD: *(smirks)* What's so bad about Grumpindor?

ELBOWS: I'm a total Snakey.

GINGER: Now all you have to do is—see that wall over there? Walk through it and you'll find all the other kids. It's even better to run though it.

> *ELBOWS lowers his head and runs right into the wall, but he doesn't pass through it. He bangs his head into the wall and falls to the floor. The family laughs.*

GINGER: What an idiot! Elbows, this is just a normal wall. The magic one is over there.

HAROLD: *(laughing uncontrollably)* He really is the worst child.

* * *

ACT I, SCENE II

* * *

PLATFORM NINE AND THREE QUARTERS

Platform Nine and Three Quarters. It looks just the same it did twenty years ago. Wizards mill about, hugging their kids. The children board the train to Hogfarts. In fact, it doesn't seem like any creative energy was put into updating this part of the world at all.

ELBOWS: I can't believe I'm finally here.

HAROLD: *(looks to GINGER)* We can't believe we can finally play tennis in the afternoons instead of looking after you.

JIMMY: Hey, look—it's unkie Romald.

> *ROMALD MEASLY (ROM for short) comes over and gives ELBOWS a noogie. Just behind him is his wife, HERHEINIE.*

ROMALD: *(continues giving ELBOWS a noogie)* Just came to see you one last time. We're all really excited for you to be somewhere else.

HAROLD: If you're really worried about not getting into Snakey, just do something really bad when you get there.

ROMALD: In other words, be yourself.

> *The family laughs. They all hate ELBOWS.*

HERHEINIE: Time to get going, little guy.

> *The adults push ELBOWS into the train's open door.*

* * *

ACT I, SCENE III

* * *

THE HOGFARTS EXPRESS

ELBOWS walks down the corridor, peeking into each carriage for somewhere to sit. He finds one he likes and goes inside. There's a blonde, pale-looking kid in it. It doesn't look like he gets outside much and he has lots of acne—SCORPIO MALFOID.

ELBOWS: Can I, uh . . . ?

SCORPIO looks up and notices how handsome ELBOWS is, pats the seat next to him, opens a bag of candy.

SCORPIO: Want some Jolly Wompers? Dummy Worms? Tooshie Drops or Guzzlers? They're made from real horses.

Another Hogfarts student peeks in the carriage, but does not enter and walks away. Then several more do the same.

ELBOWS: What's up with them?

SCORPIO: *(sighs)* You don't know who I am.

ELBOWS shakes his head.

SCORPIO: You're Elbows Patter, and I'm Scorpio Malfoid. You know the rumors.

Again, ELBOWS shakes his head.

SCORPIO: You don't? Well, I might as well tell you. The rumor is that my father, Drano Malfoid, was sterile, and used a Time Twister to turn back time and ask Moldytart to impregnate my mother. Which would make me Moldytart's son.

> *They look at each other for a moment, then explode in laughter. ELBOWS takes a Gummy Shark out of SCORPIO's candy bag and dangles it into his mouth. The magic Gummy Shark screams for help. ELBOWS swallows it whole. He is truly a monster.*

ELBOWS: That's the most ridiculous thing I ever heard. *(Pauses a moment)* You know you're pretty cute, huh.

* * *

ACT I, SCENE IV

* * *

HOGFARTS, DINING HALL

An astonishingly cliche montage of ELBOWS and SCORPIO learning magic and becoming friends, lovers, and so much more.

First is the cafeteria at Hogfarts. Students go one by one up to the front and put on the Sorting Hat, which shouts out the house they are assigned to. ELBOWS gets closer and closer to the front in line.

SORTING HAT: Grumpindor! Ravenmaw! *Hufflestuff!*

Finally, it's ELBOWS wearing the hat.

ELBOWS: Listen, hat. I'm an awful person. I forget my parents' birthdays and step on ants just to watch the world burn.

SORTING HAT:

Place my electrodes on your skull

For your magnetic sorting scan

Fear not, the current's burn is dull

In this routine electrogram

I've gazed upon the neurons in

A billion witch and wizard brains

So put me on and we'll begin

The spooky magic Sorting games…

Elbows Sevenup Patter

He puts the hat on.

Grumpin--just kidding! Snakey!

SCORPIO is next. The moment the hat touches his head:

SORTING HAT: SNAKEY!!

The action moves outside to a familiar training area, where MRS. MOOCH once trained HAROLD PATTER and his friends in broomstick flight. ELBOWS shouts at his broom.

ELBOWS: Up! Up, I said UP!

The broomstick thwacks him in the face.

MRS. MOOCH: You are without a doubt the worst student I have ever had.

SCORPIO: Up.

Without effort, he levitates the broom. He takes ELBOWS's hand and shows him how to do it right.

ELBOWS: I got it, I got it. Let me try on my own. Up!

The broom thwacks him in the face. The boys start laughing, and suddenly we are a year later, back at Platform Nine and Three Quarters. ELBOWS, with all his stuff, gives HAROLD a hug. HAROLD distances himself.

HAROLD: Alright alright, you're embarrassing me.

ELBOWS: But dad, aren't you proud of me?

HAROLD looks over his shoulder, as if someone had shouted his name.

HAROLD: Sorry, what did you say? I think someone's . . . *(he looks over his shoulder again, starts walking away)* someone's calling me. See you in eight months, kiddo!

The next year. ELBOWS hair is longer. He climbs onto the train from the platform, alone, and finds SCORPIO. They hug and kiss.

ELBOWS: Your mom?

SCORPIO shakes his head. ELBOWS reaches around and pulls SCORPIO's head into the nook of his shoulder, comforting him by running his hands through his hair.

SCORPIO: Do you think . . . *(looks up at ELBOWS)* So, I overheard my father say something about a Time Twister, it's like a clock that turns back time. They were talking about this old man, Famous Amos Dickory. They were asking if they could use the Time Twister to go back and save his son Cedar. Do you think, do you think we could go back and save my mom? I know where it is. Herheinie has it in her office.

* * *

ACT I, SCENE V

* * *

THE PATTER HOUSEHOLD

ELBOWS is sitting on his bed, making a set of beautiful, delicate homemade Christmas cards for each member of his family.

HAROLD enters and sits on the cards.

HAROLD: Hey, kiddo. I've got something for you.

ELBOWS: Dad—you're ruining them—

HAROLD: Could you try and be at least a little grateful? I didn't bring you this Christmas present so you could snap at me. Here.

> *He produces a dingy rag and tosses it in ELBOWS's face, then folds his arms petulantly.*

ELBOWS: Is this a used dish towel?

HAROLD: Well, your brother wanted the Invisibility Cloak, and your sister got some magic wings. I figured I'd better get something for you as well. I mean, I thought of this a long time ago. Not just a few minutes ago, when I remembered you were in here.

ELBOWS: Aw gee, thanks, Dad. It's really… oily.

> *HAROLD stands up, looking hurt.*

HAROLD: I should have known you'd be ungrateful.

> *He sweeps the cards, now creased from his butt, off the bed onto the floor.*

You know, there are times I wish you weren't my son. And those times are all the time.

> *HAROLD storms out, crying. ELBOWS sighs and starts collecting the fallen glitter and cards. He opens up one of the less damaged ones. In curling script on the inside, it reads, "I LOVE YOU, DAD."*

* * *

ACT I, SCENE VI

* * *

THE HOGFARTS EXPRESS

The Hogfarts Express. ELBOWS sits next to SCORPIO.

ELBOWS: My dad really hates me, I think. He said he wishes I weren't his kid.

SCORPIO: Why, because you're the worst?

ELBOWS: Yeah, I guess so.

SCORPIO: That sucks, dude.

ELBOWS: Yeah.

> *They pause, both drifting into their own angst-filled teenage worlds for a moment.*

ELBOWS: Say, how's about we bring your mom back from the dead? That'll show him I'm not the worst.

SCORPIO: Okay. But how? We don't have the Time Twister, remember?

> *ELBOWS does remember that, from a few short scenes ago. He's grateful that all the events in his life seem to take place in a laughably predictable and straightforward way.*

ELBOWS: Well, first thing's first. We gotta get off this train.

SCORPIO: But how? Look how fast we're going.

He points outside. Ambiguous Scottish countryside rolls by at an alarming speed.

ELBOWS: Don't be such a wuss.

The two get up and open a window. The wind blows in strongly. They jump out.

* * *

ACT I, SCENE VII

* * *

OLIVER SACKS' HOME FOR NEUROLOGICALLY DAMAGED WITCHES AND WIZARDS

ELBOWS and SCORPIO barge into a retirement home for wizards, not observing any of the usual visitor registration and check-in procedures. The residents are all doing things that normal, sane witches and wizards never do, like math and watching television. These are clearly the mad and infirm of the wizarding world. A NURSE walks by.

ELBOWS: Excuse me, excuse me, miss?

SCORPIO: *(mutters)* I'm not sure this is such a good idea . . .

    The NURSE acknowledges them.

NURSE: Yes?

ELBOWS: We're, um, looking for Mr. Amos Dickory. We're his um, grandsons.

NURSE: How lovely. Right this way.

    They follow the NURSE into one of the private rooms.

* * *

ACT I, SCENE VII

* * *

OLIVER SACKS' HOME FOR NEUROLOGICALLY DAMAGED WITCHES AND WIZARDS, FAMOUS AMOS'S ROOM

AMOS sits in his wheelchair, doing taxes. A young woman sits near him in a chair, knitting and listening.

AMOS: What do you think you're playing at? This isn't a game, you know. You two knuckleheads are bound to get in some big trouble with all this time travel stuff--to be honest, it doesn't even make sense! In the original books, it was impossible to change the past because in the past even your time travel to the past--had already happened!

ELBOWS and SCORPIO look at each other like, what a lunatic!

ELBOWS: We want to save your son. We've seen pictures. He's handsome.

SCORPIO: Wait, but I thought . . . you know, my mom . . .

ELBOWS: *(beaming with confidence)* We can do that too . . . if we have time.

AMOS: And how will you accomplish any of this?

ELBOWS: We know where there's a Time Twister.

For the first time, the young woman, DUMPI, looks up at them. She's pretty, her eyes blue and alight with greed.

DUMPI: Oh, do you now?

AMOS: I want nothing to do with this. Also, pretty sure this woman has cursed me into believing I'm related to her.

DUMPI puts her hand on his.

DUMPI: He is truly psychotic.

The boys nod sympathetically.

SCORPIO: Maybe you could come with us? Just so we have a classic trio?

DUMPI: *(beaming)* Of course.

* * *

ACT I, SCENE IX

* * *

PARKING LOT OUTSIDE A 7/11

ELBOWS is drinking a mysterious liquid out of a bottle.

SCORPIO: Are you sure Pollypus Potion is safe?

> *Pop! ELBOWS finishes the potion and suddenly looks like HERHEINIE. SCORPIO grabs the bottle.*

ELBOWS: I'm very sure it's not safe, in fact.

> *DUMPI snags the bottle out of SCORPIO's grip and drinks it herself. Pop! She looks like HAROLD. She pinches the fat of her new gut.*

ELBOWS/HERHEINIE: *(tests out his arms and legs)* I've always wondered what it feels like to be a woman. I could get used to this.

DUMPI/HAROLD: I've always sort of felt like a gay man.

SCORPIO: *(grabs bottle and drinks it down)* You even sound like him.

> *Pop! SCORPIO finishes the potion and transforms into ROMALD.*

SCORPIO/ROMALD: Why do my hands smell like cheese?

* * *

ACT I, SCENE X

* * *

THE MINISTRY OF MAGIC, HALLWAY

The trio walks down the hallway in their disguises, trying to act natural. They shoot finger guns at everyone they pass, and dole out a few high fives. This is cool, they think.

ELBOWS/HERHEINIE: . . . yes, yes of course. Get that memo on my desk by the end of the day.

SCORPIO/ROMALD: But I'm your husband, not your employee! Silly woman.

DUMPI/HAROLD: Good, yes. This is all totally normal. A normal day at the magic office.

They spot the real HERHEINIE and HAROLD at the end of the hall and duck inside the real HERHEINIE's office, where they suspect the Time Twister is hidden. The real HERHEINIE turns into the doorway and is blocked by SCORPIO/ROMALD, who kisses her on the mouth.

HERHEINIE: What are you doing here?

SCORPIO/ROMALD: Oh, just normal adult wizard stuff.

HERHEINIE tries to get into her office, but ROMALD blocks her.

HERHEINIE: Excuse me, you know this is my office, right? And seriously, what are you doing here? Who's running the joke shop?

SCORPIO/ROMALD: I'm uh--I'm planning a surprise for you! Roses, candles, that sort of thing. You can't look yet.

HERHEINIE: That's so sweet.

She kisses SCORPIO/ROMALD on the mouth.

HERHEINIE: But don't think it'll get you out of couples therapy on Wednesday. We're never going to work through our problems if you don't put in an effort.

* * *

ACT I, SCENE XI

* * *

THE MINISTRY OF MAGIC, HERHEINIE'S OFFICE

Back in HERHEINE's office, the Pollypus Potion is wearing off. DUMPI, SCORPIO, and ELBOWS all let out horrible screams of agony as they transform back into themselves.

SCORPIO: So, where do you think the Time Twister is?

ELBOWS: Well, Herheinie loves puzzles, because she's a huge nerd. We'll probably have to solve some complicated riddle to get to it.

SCORPIO: I can respect that.

> *Suddenly, a painting of a STUDIOUS WIZARD on the wall clears its throat.*

STUDIOUS WIZARD:

If it's the Time Twister you seek,

Around this room you'll have to—

DUMPI: *Crucioblammo!*

> *The STUDIOUS WIZARD starts screaming, in horrible pain. DUMPI grins insanely as she holds the torture curse. SCORPIO and ELBOWS exchange eyebrow raises like, yikes.*

STUDIOUS WIZARD: Ahhh! Fine, I'll tell you! Please, God, stop! It's in the third desk drawer! The safe combination is 14-9-3! Oh God, it hurts, please, please, stop!

DUMPI: That's what I thought.

She lowers her wand. The STUDIOUS WIZARD collapses into broken sobs as DUMPI heads to the desk.

ELBOWS: Uh, that was…

SCORPIO: You really had no hesitations about torturing that guy, huh?

ELBOWS: Yeah, you really went for it. Like, immediately.

DUMPI: Well, you know. Girl's gotta do what a girl's gotta do.

SCORPIO: I guess. You probably didn't have to—

DUMPI: Got it!

She's already opened the safe and is holding up the Time Twister.

DUMPI: Now we can go back and restore Moldytart to the—uhh, I mean, save my hot nephew.

ELBOWS: Again, this plan seems totally fine.

Arm in arm, they skip out of the office.

ACT II

* * *

ACT II, SCENE I

* * *

THE EDGE OF THE SPOOKY FOREST

ELBOWS and DUMPI throw a football back and forth. ELBOWS throws a perfect spiral.

DUMPI: You're getting it!

ELBOWS: You're like the dad I never had. Er, the dad who knows how to throw a football I never had.

> *ELBOWS throws another perfect spiral and stares into DUMPI's eyes.*

SCORPIO: I've figured out how we can save Cedar, if anyone's still--

ELBOWS: *(interrupts)* I've got it! We can use the Time Twister to travel back to the Triwizard Tournament and make sure that Cedar loses, so he never faces Moldytart with Harold.

DUMPI: Oh, Elbows. What a brilliant plan.

SCORPIO: Exactly. I read up on this, and it seems like Cedric used magic to distract the dragon, so if--

ELBOWS: *(interrupts)* So if we disarm him just before that, he'll--

SCORPIO: *(now interrupting)* --lose. I've been thinking about it, and only Elbows and I should go back.

DUMPI: Why? 'cause I'm a girl?

SCORPIO: No, because you're . . .

ELBOWS: Scorpio is right, Dumpi. You shouldn't come.

SCORPIO: I am?

ELBOWS: Dumpi, you've never been a Hogwarts student, you won't know how to play the part.

DUMPI: *(sullen)* You're right. Good luck, boys.

> *She kisses ELBOWS on the cheek and hands him the Time Twister. ELBOWS and SCORPIO hold onto it while the dial spins, slow at first, then faster and faster as time slows down, then stops, then rewinds faster and faster and faster until there is a great white flash of light.*

* * *

ACT II, SCENE II

* * *

TRIWIZARD TOURNAMENT, EDGE OF THE SPOOKY FOREST, 1994

We are back at the Triwizard Tournament that took place in the fourth book. It's almost as if everything ELBOWS and SCORPIO did came back to the plot of the original books, with nothing new added.

The announcer, BUDO LAGMAN projects his voice across the stands:

BUDO LAGMAN: Weeeeeeeeeelcome ladies, gents, and all the rest of you gender-identifiers, to a plodding retread of the original books!

The crowd goes wild.

BUDO LAGMAN: Can I hear a *HOGFARTS?*

The Hogfarts crowd cheers.

BUDO LAGMAN: Can I hear a *GERMAN EQUIVALENT OF HOGFARTS?*

The German crowd cheers.

BUDO LAGMAN: Can I hear a *FRENCH EQUIVALENT OF HOGFARTS?*

There is no cheer.

SCORPIO: Look, nobody has cellphones. It must be 1994.

BUDO LAGMAN: Wizaaaaaaaards and witches, allow me to introduce, contestant number one, number one seed *SOME*

GERMAN GUY! From the French equivalent to Hogfarts, we've got *SOME FRENCH GIRL!* And, finally, from Hogfarts itself, the host with the most, we've got no fewer than TWO contestants: first, the handsome, the dashing, *CEDAR DICKORY.* And last, but not least-- well, maybe seeded last, the boy who lived, *HAROLD PATTER!* Check out those dragons they're facing, those are some mean critters!

> *The dragons groan and bellow. Each of the contestants swoops down on a broomstick, trying to steal the egg from their dragon's nest.*

BUDO LAGMAN: Look at that Cedar go!

SCORPIO: Elbows, we're running out of time. Remember, Dumpi said we only had five minutes.

> *CEDAR swerves and ducks under the dragon's firebreath.*

ELBOWS: *(quiet)* Expelliwammo!

> *CEDAR's wand is flung aside, and he is left defenseless as the dragon chases after him.*

BUDO LAGMAN: Looks like Cedar's out of this one before it even really starts. Poor kid, but a good jawline doesn't always make for good brains, if you know what I mean.

CROWD: *(in unison)* WE ACTUALLY DON'T KNOW WHAT YOU MEAN, AND THAT SOUNDS KIND OF PREJUDICED AND, FRANKLY, OFFENSIVE.

> *A flash of white. Time spins forward, and we are back in the present. ELBOWS shrieks in pain. HAROLD, GINGER, DRANO, surround the kids, but now they all have different hairstyles, different clothes. Something has changed.*

ELBOWS: Did it work?

> *ELBOWS passes out.*

* * *

ACT II, SCENE III

* * *

HOGFARTS, HOSPITAL

ELBOWS is still unconscious, now lying in a hospital bed. HAROLD sits next to the bed, consulting the painting of ELBOWS MUMBLEDORE on the wall.

HAROLD: It's been a long time, Professor Mumbledore.

MUMBLEDORE: How is the boy doing?

HAROLD: They say he'll recover, but something seems wrong. *(pauses)* Can I ask you something?

MUMBLEDORE: Shoot.

HAROLD: How do you feel about me naming him after you?

MUMBLEDORE: Well, to be frank, Harold, it's a little embarrassing. He is kind of the worst, isn't he?

> *HAROLD nods gravely. ELBOWS jolts awake, and when HAROLD looks back up at the portrait, MUMBLEDORE is gone.*

ELBOWS: Where am I?

HAROLD: You're in the hospital. Do you know how worried I was?

ELBOWS: What happened?

HAROLD: I want you stay away from that Scorpio boy, he's no good. You shouldn't be running around with . . . you know.

ELBOWS: I know what?

HAROLD: You know, a Snakey.

ELBOWS: But I'm a Snakey!

HAROLD shakes his head.

HAROLD: Let's get you tested for a concussion, kiddo. And I *forbid* you from hanging out with Scorpio. I'll have my friends here watch you, keep the two of you in separate classes.

ELBOWS looks stricken as HAROLD exits.

* * *

ACT II, SCENE IV

* * *

HOGFARTS, STAIRCASE

ELBOWS chases after his dad HAROLD.

ELBOWS: You can't stop me from being with Scorpio, we're meant to be together. We'll run away.

HAROLD: Elbows, enough.

> *ROMALD meets them in the stairs. He looks different now: different hair, worse shoes.*

ELBOWS: Uncle Romald, tell my dad he can't stop me being friends with Scorpio. I could really use one of your pranks right now.

ROMALD: Pranks? I was on my way to find Padme, have you seen her around? Pranks. I could use a prank or two.

ELBOWS: From your prank shop.

ROMALD: Prank shop?

ELBOWS: And who's this Padme, anyway?

HAROLD: *(concerned)* She's Romald's new girlfriend, don't you remember?

ROMALD: You forgot Aunt Padme? You know, Padme, my son Anakin's mom?

ELBOWS: But you're married to Herheinie!

ROMALD and HAROLD look at each other and laugh hysterically.

HAROLD: Sounds like quite a concussion. He forgot that he's in Grumpindor House as well.

ELBOWS: But how? I always knew I would be Snakey.

ROMALD: Anakin dared you, don't you remember? He said you couldn't get into Grumpindor even if you tried, so you did.

They run into SCORPIO on the stairs.

SCORPIO: Oh, Elbows, it's so good to see you!

They hug and kiss.

ELBOWS: I'm sorry. I'm sorry, Scorpio, but we can't hang out anymore.

SCORPIO: But—why? I'm so relieved to see you.

ELBOWS pushes him away. He whispers into SCORPIO's ear:

ELBOWS: My dad, he . . . I just, I just can't.

* * *

ACT II, SCENE V

* * *

DEFENSE AGAINST THE DARK ARTS CLASSROOM

ELBOWS is late to class, so he tries to tiptoe in without making any sound. There is a wild-haired woman at the front of the classroom, drawing a pentagram on the chalkboard with jerky movements.

As ELBOWS sits down, his chair squeaks. The teacher spins around: It's HERHEINIE. She's not wearing any makeup, and her face is sallow and wrathful.

HERHEINIE: Late. Again.

ELBOWS: Whoa. Uh—sorry, Herheinie.

HERHEINIE: It's Professor Danger.

ELBOWS: Don't you mean Danger-Measly?

> *The class giggles.*

HERHEINIE: SILENCE!

> *The students quiet immediately.*

HERHEINIE: Ten points from Grumpindor, Mr. Potter, for the suggestion that I would be married to any useless man, let alone Romald Measly, the *most* useless man.

> *She huffs and turns back to the blackboard, where she's drawn the standard male sex symbol at the center of the pentagram and is writing out a curse.*

ANAKIN MEASLY, ROM and PADME's son, leans over and whispers in ELBOWS's ear.

ANAKIN: See, my dad rejected her back when they were in school, and then she turned into a total witch. You wouldn't have guessed it, but seems like when it came down to it, all the happiness in her life rested on one man's approval.

ELBOWS: Wow. What about all her ambitions? She was such a multifaceted, nuanced person. You know, back in the day.

ANAKIN shrugs.

HERHEINIE *(to the class):* … and you'll all be tested on this today, at the end of class. Learn quick, kiddos.

All the students take notes.

HERHEINIE: And as far as my "ambitions," Mr. Patter . . .

She turns to face ELBOWS, whose eyes go wide. She heard him.

HERHEINIE: … A hundred points from Grumpindor. How's that for ambitions?

ELBOWS groans. The bell rings and he gets out of there as fast as he can.

* * *

ACT II, SCENE VI

* * *

HOGFARTS, STAIRCASES

SCORPIO, looking glum, walks down the staircase and runs into who else but DUMPI.

DUMPI: Hey! How are ya?

SCORPIO: What are you doing here? It's nice to see you, but how did you get in?

DUMPI: Security's pretty chill, once you've knocked out the protective charms and guard dogs and all that.

SCORPIO: You did what?

DUMPI: How about these moving staircases? Wow.

SCORPIO: Yeah, they're cool. Where did you go to school, anyway?

DUMPI: Oh, I was homeschooled mostly. I was a sick kid most of the time, so different schools here and there.

    SCORPIO casts his eyes down.

SCORPIO: Oh. I didn't know.

DUMPI: Look, we need to fix it. What we did in the past didn't work. Cedar still died--he had no problem defeating the dragon without a wand, and ended up winning with Harold.

SCORPIO: I know, I know. We screwed up. It's just, Elbows-- honestly, he's the worst sometimes. He can't help it.

DUMPI: That's not what I'm saying. I'm saying we need to give it another chance.

* * *

ACT II, SCENE VII

* * *

HOGFARTS, LIBRARY

ELBOWS is perusing the "SELF-HELP AND RELATIONSHIPS" aisle of the library when SCORPIO pokes his head out from behind a shelf.

SCORPIO: Psst! Elbows, over here.

ELBOWS: What are you doing here? My dad said we couldn't make out anymore, remember.

SCORPIO: I'm not here for that--well, not *only* for that. Haven't you noticed how weird everything is? Like, Romald doesn't run a joke shop anymore?

ELBOWS: Actually, I was wondering about that. Doesn't it seem strange to you that Romald grew up to run a joke shop? Whenever my dad talks about him and Romald when they were at Hogfarts, it was Romald's older brothers who ran the joke shop--he never had anything to do with that.

> *It's almost as if nobody bothered to imagine what Romald might actually grow up to do.*

SCORPIO: Let's not dwell on that.

> *Or considered how inconsistent the rules of magic are in this universe.*

SCORPIO: Look, remember how when our parents were at Hogfarts that journalist Ratty Schemer wrote about everything that happened in their lives? I really conveniently found this cool book that lists every decision our parents ever made, their reasons for making it, and the consequences of each one.

ELBOWS: So? How does that help us?

SCORPIO: It'll tell us exactly where we need to change time to make everything go back to normal. And to bring my mom back.

ELBOWS: You mean Cedar Dickory.

SCORPIO: No, I--I feel like you're forgetting the whole point of this mission.

ELBOWS: I mean, a mission can have, like, points and sub-points.

SCORPIO: Okay, whatever. Anyway, we can still change things. We just have to--

ELBOWS: Look, read Ratty Schemer's book. In this reality, the one we're standing in now, Herheinie was supposed to go to the ball with Igor Kram, but she bailed at the last minute because she was spooked by what happened when we expelliwhammoed Cedar's wand at the games! Instead she just stayed at home and ate peanut butter, not that there's anything wrong with that.

SCORPIO: It's important to combat body dysmorphia at every step.

ELBOWS: After that night, everything was changed from our timeline. She never got together with Romald. So we have to go back a *second* time, and expelliwhammo ourselves, to undo our undoing of what we undid.

SCORPIO: No, remember what Dumpi said? It's too dangerous to meddle with the same patch of time over and over again. We have to find another moment in this extremely delicate timeline to disrupt.

ELBOWS: Okay… then I think I might have another idea.

SCORPIO: Does it involve time-travel? Please say it doesn't involve time travel.

ELBOWS: Do you have the Time Twister?

SCORPIO: If I give it to you, promise no more time travel.

ELBOWS: I promise: no more schmime schmavel.

SCORPIO gives him the Time Twister.

SCORPIO: Now what do we do?

ELBOWS: We go back in time, bozo! We need to make Cedar lose again.

SCORPIO: And how do you plan to do that?

ELBOWS: I'll explain everything. But first, we have to find the girls' washroom.

SCORPIO: You want to make out in the girls' washroom?

ELBOWS: That's not actually what I had in mind. But yes. I'd be down for that.

ELBOWS pinches SCORPIO's butt as they leave the library.

* * *

ACT II, SCENE VIII

* * *

HOGFARTS, GIRLS' BATHROOM

SCORPIO and ELBOWS enter the girls' bathroom.

ELBOWS: Gross! Smells like ladies!

SCORPIO: So, we're gonna go back in time to the Triwizard Tournament again, wait for the *third* event, where Cedar was swimming underwater, and cast a spell to make his head four times as big so that it floats and brings him to the surface? I don't understand, how does making it four times larger--

ELBOWS: *(interrupts)* No time for questions! Practice the spell.

SCORPIO: *(points his wand at ELBOWS's face)* Engorgiblammo!

> *ELBOWS's head quadruples in size.*

SCORPIO: Look, now go in the bathtub. It doesn't make any sense, the size of your head . . .

ELBOWS: There's no time!

SCORPIO: And how are we even getting underwater?

> *A gush of water comes out of the bathtub spigot, followed by MARITIME MARTLE.*

MARITIME MARTLE: Why, hello boys.

ELBOWS: What's cookin', good lookin'?

MARITIME MARTLE: What a flatterer!

ELBOWS: Anyways, we were hoping we could take a trip down your pipes.

MARITIME MARTLE: Oooh, you don't say! Come inside.

> *ELBOWS and SCORPIO dive after her into the pipes. ELBOWS spins the Time Twister. Time slows, stills, and spools backward into the decades.*
>
> *Just as the boys disappear, HAROLD, GINGER, DRANO, and PROFESSOR MAGOGANALLAGALL run into the room.*

HAROLD: They're gone. Where'd they go, Martle? Martle, I know you're in there.

> *She reappears.*

MARITIME MARTLE: Someone's looking handsome in their big boy clothes.

DRANO: Myrtle! Where did they go?

MARITIME MARTLE: Not a question of where . . .

HAROLD: Then it must be a question of . . . when.

* * *

ACT II, SCENE IX

* * *

TRIWIZARD TOURNAMENT, LAKE, 1995

BUDO LAGMAN: Witches and wizards, flora and fauna--all you single-cellular organisms out there--allow me to welcome you to the annual Triwizard Tournament!

> *The crowd cheers. Somehow, the scene is exactly as it was in the fourth book. It's almost as if the writers couldn't come up with anything and decided to just reuse scenes and settings from the books.*

> *ELBOWS and SCORPIO swim through the lake.*

BUDO LAGMAN: Let's all cheer for our four contestants--remember it's that German guy, that French girl, and from the home team, Hogfarts itself--Cedar Dickory and Harold Patter.

> *CEDAR DICKORY swims toward ELBOWS and SCORPIO underwater.*

BUDO LAGMAN: They're on a race to save their loved ones, and it looks like that German kid has turned himself into a cute lil tadpole, Harold Patter is all gilled up, and Cedar Dickory has created some kind of air bubble around his head.

ELBOWS: *(whispers)* Engorgiblammo!

> *CEDAR starts to grow. His whole body gets larger and larger. It is unclear why making him bigger will make him float, when it seems like the ratio of air to body weight will remain the same. Anyway, he floats to the top of the lake.*

BUDO LAGMAN: What a disaster! What a shame! Cedar Dickory is no longer underwater, he's lost the competition for sure, he's floating up into the air, up, up into the sky--wonder if we'll ever see him again-- he's floating up through the atmosphere, through the ozone, and into outer space. Well I never saw a thing like that before, a boy float right up into space--sure is a magical world we all live in.

ELBOWS and SCORPIO fist-bump.

Time speeds up, at first a little, then faster and faster until there's a huge white flash and we're back in the present.

SCORPIO breaks through the surface of lake and laughs.

SCORPIO: We did it, Elbows. You and me, we did it.

He looks around for ELBOWS.

SCORPIO: Elbows?

THESAURUS DRAWBRIDGE: Get out of the lake this INSTANT.

He climbs out.

SCORPIO: Excuse me, lady, I'm looking for my friend.

THESAURUS DRAWBRIDGE: Lady? And exactly who do you think you're talking to? I'm Professor Drawbridge, headmistress of Hogfarts.

SCORPIO: But, but . . .

THESAURUS DRAWBRIDGE: You think just because you're a *Malfoid*, you can do whatever you like? What were you doing in the lake?

SCORPIO: Looking for my friend . . . do you know where he is? Elbows. His name is Elbows Patter.

THESAURUS DRAWBRIDGE: Ridiculous! Have you lost your mind, boy? The last Patter must have been . . . was it Harold? Oh, that petulant, stupid boy. He was truly the worst child, or at least until I met you.

SCORPIO: Where is he?

THESAURUS DRAWBRIDGE: *(laughs)* Harold Patter has been dead since before you were born.

> *A gust of wind. Dark shapes take form around SCORPIO. They are DeMentos, black spirits that suck out the life of overeager boys and girls and mix it with soda to make a big fizzy overflowing thing.*

THESAURUS DRAWBRIDGE: Do you need medical attention? Have you forgotten your name? First you don't know who I am, and now you don't know that Harold Patter's dead! He was part of that old grouch Mumbledore's army of terrorists we defeated--thank god--at the Battle of the Bands of Hogfarts. Let's get moving, the DeMentos are getting all riled up and hungry, and you've done your absolute best to spoil my favorite day of the year--Moldytart Day.

SCORPIO: Moldytart Day?

ACT III

* * *

ACT III, SCENE I

* * *

HOGFARTS, HEADMISTRESS'S OFFICE

SCORPIO sits across a wooden desk from THESAURUS DRAWBRIDGE.

THESAURUS DRAWBRIDGE: Scorpio, I have to admit I'm a little concerned.

> *She pauses briefly.*

THESAURUS DRAWBRIDGE: You've always been a standout student. Great with the ladies, even better with the snatch. In Quiddurch, that is. You've helped me, immensely, to weed out those last Mumbledore supports among the students.

SCORPIO: I . . . I did a good job at that, yeah? Got rid of lots of those dumb old Mumbledore supporters?

> *From offstage, we hear the faint shrieks of a girl being tortured, perhaps being told she is chubby.*

THESAURUS DRAWBRIDGE: I have to ask, though. What happened with the lake? You were a model fascist, and now you're asking questions about that pitiful rebel Harold Patter . . . what's going on, Scorpio?

SCORPIO: Oh, you know. Clunked my head against a doorway again! Always doing that. Just an ordinary, non-magical concussion doing normal person things.

THESAURUS DRAWBRIDGE: I see. So you'll continue to report any students with . . . subversive views.

SCORPIO: One hundo percent. Totally gonna keep doing that.

She extends a hand; he shakes it.

THESAURUS DRAWBRIDGE: For Moldytart and Mallard.

SCORPIO: For moldy farts and cowards.

* * *

ACT III, SCENE II

* * *

HOGFARTS, GROUNDS

LARS JENKUM: Heyo! Check it out--it's the Porpoise King! What's the haps, Porpoise King?

He fist-bumps SCORPIO.

LARS JENKUM: See you tomorrow after sun-down. Let's go get those Funbloods!

LARS JENKUM walks off, hooting and laughing.

HOLLY CHAPSTICK comes up behind SCORPIO and taps him in the shoulder.

HOLLY CHAPSTICK: Hey there, cutie pie. So are you gonna ask me already?

SCORPIO: Me? Oh, yeah. I'm the cute Porpoise King, totally understand what that means. Wait, ask you to what?

HOLLY CHAPSTICK: The Blood Bath, silly! Remember? You're the Porpoise King, and maybe I could be your date . . .

From offstage we hear shrieks.

SCORPIO: Maybe a silly question, but what are all those screams about? Like, I totally know, but could you remind me? Totally chill about the screams.

HOLLY CHAPSTICK: The Funbloods, of course. You're the one who--oh, gross: I got Funblood all over my socks! Not again!

She licks a finger and smudges the blood, only making it worse.

HOLLY CHAPSTICK: Anywho, like the Mallard says, everyone hates a Funblood, so let's go to the Blood Ball together. For Moldytart and Mallard.

SCORPIO: Like, mallards the bird . . . ?

Holly giggles.

HOLLY CHAPSTICK: Oh, Porpoise King. You're so funny!

She kisses him on the cheek, then darts off.

* * *

ACT III, SCENE III

* * *

MINISTRY OF MAGIC, OFFICE OF THE HEAD OF MAGICAL LAW ENFORCEMENT

DRANO sits behind a huge, ornate desk. He wears elaborate robes. All around his office is the insignia of the Mallard.

DRANO: What took you so long, slowpoke?

SCORPIO: I didn't know where you--oh, just normal wizard problems, you know. Long line at the fireplace. Totally knew where I was going.

DRANO: Are you not ashamed?

SCORPIO: Totally know what you're talking about, but could you remind me? Just to like, refresh.

DRANO: What about all these questions you're asking, about Harold Patter? It's a travesty!

SCORPIO: *(stands up)* It's you! Are you the one ordering the Funbloods rounded up, torturing everyone, ushering in a world of dark magic and destruction?

DRANO nods.

SCORPIO: Well, great. Because I was gonna say this alternate reality is actually pretty sick.

* * *

ACT III, SCENE IV

* * *

HOGFARTS, LIBRARY

SCORPIO goes through all the books--he's looking for something, then finds it. He opens it up and starts reading.

SCORPIO: What happened, all those years? What made this world so dope?

DOUG BAKER: Uh, hello? What are you doing here, Porpoise King?

SCORPIO: I'm reading.

DOUG BAKER: Look, I'm sorry I haven't finished the paper yet, but I'll have it to you tomorrow I swear.

SCORPIO: Paper?

DOUG BAKER: No one's more chill than the Porpoise King. Biggest paper of the year for Professor Grape, and you don't even remember about it. I'm writing for you, free of charge--you're such a chill, likeable, and handsome guy.

SCORPIO: Oh, yeah. Of course. So chill.

DOUG BAKER: *(walks away, chanting)* Porpoise King! Porpoise King!

All the students in the library cheer.

STUDENTS: PORPOISE KING!

* * *

ACT III, SCENE V

* * *

HOGFARTS, LOTIONS CLASSROOM

SCORPIO opens the door and runs inside without knocking.

SCORPIO: Sevenup Grape, Sevenup Grape!

GRAPE: I'm actually Professor Grape, in case you forgot. I've heard some strange things about you lately, Porpoise King.

SCORPIO: Yes, well. I need--do you still work for Mumbledore?

GRAPE: Work for Mumbledore? Mumbledore's been dead for twenty years.

SCORPIO: I know you were secretly on his side. You have to believe me, crazy as it sounds, but there's this alternate reality where Moldytart lost the Battle of Hogfarts.

GRAPE: Sounds like you've had a few too many Funbloody marys.

SCORPIO: Listen, we had a Time Twister. I met this girl, this wonderful girl Dumpi Diggory. Her uncle Cedar Dickory died at the last Triwizard Tournament, so me and my friend Elbows went back in time to save him. We made him lose, so he wouldn't face Moldytart with Harold Patter, so he'd survive. But now everything's different. I'm the Porpoise King, girls are talking to me.

GRAPE: This is quite a nice story, but I know what you're doing. You're trying to get me to admit something, but I've done nothing wrong. Nothing wrong against Moldytart, for certain.

SCORPIO: I know . . . I know you were in love with Lippy Patter! Harold's mother!

GRAPE gives him a serious look, then grabs his cape and leads the way out of the room.

GRAPE: Follow me.

They duck into a secret passage that opens at the back of the classroom.

* * *

ACT III, SCENE VI

* * *

CAMPAIGN ROOM

The moment SCORPIO walks in the room, HERHEINIE slams him into a wall. Her hair is cut short, her clothing is in tatters. All in all, she looks pretty dope.

HERHEINIE: Just give me a reason. One reason.

GRAPE: It's okay, he's with us. Everybody just relax. I can explain.

> *HERHEINIE keeps him against the wall.*

SCORPIO: It's true. I'm from an alternate reality. Me and Elbows got our hands on a Time Twister--

HERHEINIE: Elbows Mumbledore?

> *ROMALD walks in, picking his nose. Then, spotting SCORPIO, pulls out his wand. Confetti shoots out of it.*

ROMALD: Blimey. Accidentally grabbed my trick wand again.

> *Looks like, in spite of the seriousness of the circumstances, ROMALD is still really into jokes in this alternate reality. Makes total sense.*

SCORPIO: I'm on your side! Listen, listen. I can explain.

GRAPE: *(shakes head)* He's talking about a different Elbows.

HERHEINIE: What do you mean, "a different Elbows"?

SCORPIO: Look, maybe you should all just sit down.

* * *

ACT III, SCENE VII

* * *

CAMPAIGN ROOM

HERHEINIE is pensively sharpening a dagger, and ROM sits slack-jawed as they take it all in.

ROM: That's quite the story, Porpoise King.

HERHEINIE: I believe him. No way he could know all of that stuff except by being from an alternate timeline.

SCORPIO: So, can you help me? This reality is honestly pretty cool, but I feel pretty bad about erasing Elbows from existence and all that.

ROM: You've come to the right people. Me, Grape, and Danger here are pretty much all that's left of Mumbledore's Army. Really just the dregs.

HERHEINIE: So, this other world, before you messed it up... Moldytart is dead?

SCORPIO: Yeah, totally. Most of your friends are still alive. You're Minister for Magic.

ROM: I always felt like I was destined for something great.

SCORPIO: No, Herheinie. Also, you guys are married.

    ROM stammers. HERHEINIE blushes and sharpens her knife faster.

ROM: Well, that's--uh--

HERHEINIE: Really interesting stuff--

ROM: Oh, yeah. Super crazy.

HERHEINIE: I, um.

ROM: Yikes.

HERHEINIE: Him and me? Ha.

ROM: Yikeroo.

SCORPIO: Oh, and Grape is dead.

HERHEINIE: What, us? In love? Psh.

ROM: So absurd.

HERHEINIE: Pretty wack, right?

GRAPE: *(voice breaking)* H--how was I killed?

SCORPIO: You were brutally murdered. By Moldytart.

ROM: Can you believe that? Us, married. What a laugh!

HERHEINIE: Can't even imagine.

> *They both laugh awkwardly, avoiding eye contact with one another, as GRAPE stands horrified, trying to process the knowledge of his own gruesome death.*

GRAPE: This is traumatizing.

ROM: You're telling me!

SCORPIO: Okay, anyway, now that we've all moved on, I think we should come up with a plan. So, it seems like our best bet is to go back and block the charms we used on Cedar in the first and second tasks. We'll only have a few minutes.

> *ROM clears his throat and pulls out a map.*

ROM: Okay, yeah. No need to make things awkward. Let's just focus on the plan.

He unrolls the map and points to a spot on the far side of the lake.

ROM: This is where the first task happened. We'll have to go here first, then to the other side to block the second charm.

HERHEINIE: I'll go with Porpoise King.

GRAPE: Are you sure that's a good idea? There are WANTED: DEAD OR ALIVE posters with your face on them everywhere. It'll be dangerous.

HERHEINIE: You're right. We should all go.

ROM: Makes sense to me.

> *The four of them hold hands and program the Time Twister for 1994. Time dissolves with a bunch of fun onomatopoeias, whooshing and swirling backwards in big bouncing loops. You know, like time travel.*

* * *

ACT III, SCENE VIII

* * *

EDGE OF THE SPOOKY FOREST, 1994

For like the third time in the play, we see the same scene that we also saw unfold in the fourth book. In spite of the unapologetic recycling of material, this all feels fresh to us. Oh, look, it's Budo Lagman again. What a surprise.

BUDO LAGMAN: Iiiiit's Cedar Dickoryyyy! Look at him go. Really, uh… really taking on that dragon in a compelling way. So cool.

GRAPE: Come on, we need to move. The Time Twister is already spinning back.

BUDO LAGMAN: Boy, it sure is a treat to watch all this stuff happen. So exciting, ladiewitches and gentlewizards.

> *ELBOWS tries to cast his meddlesome charm, but HERHEINIE disarms him just in time. ELBOWS looks confused.*

> *Then, the Time Twister pulls them back into its vortex of trouble, and they're spit back out into the present.*

* * *

ACT III, SCENE IX

* * *

EDGE OF THE SPOOKY FOREST

They're back in the present. Funblood screams echo faintly in the distance. SCORPIO still can't believe how badass this place is.

ROM doubles over in pain.

ROM: Ow! Ow, the Time Twister hurt me!

HERHEINIE: What? How? What happened? The plan didn't work.

ROM: I don't know, I can't describe it. It's just a vague sort of agony.

> *He moves on entirely, and there are zero consequences. It's almost like this whole pain thing is just a halfhearted attempt to make the mechanics of the Time Twister more interesting.*

SCORPIO: Wait, we're on the wrong side of the lake. We have to get across if we're going to--

> *Suddenly, somebody turns up the air conditioning in the theater to full blast. We instinctively know what this icy chill means: evil.*

> *DeMentos glide in from the aisles, climbing onstage to join our characters. It looks cool, somehow.*

GRAPE: We're out of time.

HERHEINIE: Go. I'll sacrifice myself so you guys can get away.

ROM: Okay.

They all start to leave.

HERHEINIE: Wait. I just want to say… Rom, you're, uh… hot. I've always thought so. Just. Going on the record here.

ROM: Oh, Herheinie. You're kinda hot too.

They kiss.

SCORPIO: Okay, guys, we should really get out of here if we want to--

It's too late. The DeMentos are on them. They grab ROM and HERHEINIE and pull them apart, then lean in and suck out their souls. It is disgusting.

GRAPE: Stay calm. They won't attack us. We're on their side. *(To the DeMentos)* We're cool, guys.

The head DeMento gives GRAPE a thumbs-up.

THESAURUS DRAWBRIDGE walks on. The DeMentos salute her.

THESAURUS DRAWBRIDGE: Kissasses. Cut that out.

The DeMentos ease up.

Well. Grape and the Porpoise King. What brings the two of you out here? With these… fugitives?

GRAPE: What? Oh! You're right. There they are, huh? What a weird coincidence. No clue how they got there.

THESAURUS DRAWBRIDGE: Nice try, Grape. I know you're a double agent working for Mumbledore's Army.

GRAPE: How long have you suspected?

THESAURUS DRAWBRIDGE: For years. DeMentos, attack!

The DeMentos fall on GRAPE. He screams as they take his soul.

SCORPIO: Um…

THESAURUS DRAWBRIDGE: Oh, Porpoise King. We all owe you a debt of gratitude for leading us to these rebels. They were the last of the resistance. Now, thanks to you, there's no one left to prevent us from ruling the world forever. You're a hero.

SCORPIO starts to object, but then looks around and reconsiders his options.

SCORPIO: Yeah, you know what, it's no problem. Just saving the day, as usual. No need to thank me.

THESAURUS DRAWBRIDGE: You can have anything you want.

SCORPIO: A feast in my honor?

THESAURUS DRAWBRIDGE: We'll break out the Funblood bone china.

SCORPIO: Sweet!

They shake hands, then:

SCORPIO AND THESAURUS: For Moldytart and Mallards!

The DeMentos cheer and pick up SCORPIO on their shoulders, crowd surfing him around.

DEMENTOS *(all, chanting):* PORPOISE KING! PORPOISE KING! PORPOISE KING!

SCORPIO: I could get used to this.

* * *

ACT III, SCENE X

* * *

HOGFARTS, DINING HALL

It's the annual Blood Bath ball. Every Hogfarts student sits at their table, banqueting on lobster and champagne with a drop of Funblood. At the front of the room, three Funblood students are tied to the bass of an enormous chocolate fondue fountain, scalding them.

SCORPIO, wearing a porpoise costume, holds HOLLY CHAPSTICK's hand at the front of the room. He raises his glass.

SCORPIO: *(shouts)* A toast!

HOGFARTS STUDENTS *(in unison)*: A toast!

> *HOLLY CHAPSTICK looks up at SCORPIO, beaming.*

SCORPIO: To this totally dope alternate reality!

> *The crowd cheers. They have no idea what he's talking about, but they love the Porpoise King. He kisses HOLLY CHAPSTICK on the mouth. The crowd cheers louder.*
>
> *THESAURUS DRAWBRIDGE, standing at the far end of the hall, uses magic to project her voice.*

THESAURUS DRAWBRIDGE: I officially proclaim Scorpio Malfoid the coolest kid in school!

> *All the Hogfarts students pour onstage to join in the celebration, and SCORPIO is showered with gifts from his admiring fans--bouquets of flowers, Funblood organs, and confetti.*

SCORPIO: Let's get this party started!

All the thousands of students in the hall climb up onto the long tables. They take each other's hands, shout along with the music, and dance. We can see that he's finally found the place he belongs. They are young, and know magic, and it feels like the party will never end. ELBOWS, his mother, and CEDAR DICKORY all but forgotten, SCORPIO loses himself in the revelry of this dope new world.

About the Author

John Marquane started his writing career as one of the least funny members of the Harvard Lampoon, where his writing was described by his parents as "interesting" and "not particularly funny." In the years since graduating college, John Marquane wrote several literary novels under the pseudonym "Jonathan Safran Foer" to support his true passion: parody novels. In addition to *Harold Patter and the Worst Child*, he has published a parody of *The Catcher in the Rye* in the voice of Donald J. Trump titled *The Candidate in the Rye*.

Made in the USA
Lexington, KY
14 October 2016